THE SALVATION ARMY IN THE BODY OF CHRIST

AN ECCLESIOLOGICAL STATEMENT

A statement issued by the International Headquarters of The Salvation Army by authority of the General, in consultation with the International Doctrine Council and the International Management Council

THE SALVATION ARMY IN THE BODY OF CHRIST

An Ecclesiological Statement

Salvation Books
The Salvation Army International Headquarters
London, United Kingdom

First published 2008

Copyright © 2008
The General of The Salvation Army

ISBN 978-0-85412-774-0

Published by Salvation Books
The Salvation Army International Headquarters
101 Queen Victoria Street, London EC4V 4EH
United Kingdom

Printed by UK Territory Print & Design Unit

CONTENTS

FOREWORD

I am pleased and privileged to introduce to Salvationists everywhere this Statement of where The Salvation Army stands within the Body of Christ. It has been through multiple stages of preparation and I record deep thanks to the many who have contributed to it, not least the members of the International Doctrine Council under their Chairperson, Commissioner William Francis, and the members of the International Management Council at International Headquarters in London. Both of these Councils, by reason of their multi-ethnic memberships, represent attitudes and insights of a global nature.

The Statement is intended to be useful to all Salvationists in understanding our place among the many churches, denominations, para-church bodies, church councils and other Christian groups that exist around the world. It will be especially useful to those of us who are actively engaged in ecumenical relations and can readily be shared with others beyond our ranks if this will be an aid to mutual understanding. The Statement is not intended to say new things, but its purpose is to clarify and consolidate present global thinking on our identity within the wider Body of Christ.

May God bless and use this short publication to his lasting glory and may the Army always be ready to obey his leadings, remaining a permanent mission to the unconverted as well as a modern, even unique, expression of church life.

Shaw Clifton
General
April 2008

SUMMARY STATEMENT

1. The Body of Christ on earth (also referred to in this paper as the Church universal) comprises all believers in Jesus Christ as Saviour and Lord.

2. Believers stand in a spiritual relationship to one another, which is not dependent upon any particular church structure.

3. The Salvation Army, under the one Triune God, belongs to and is an expression of the Body of Christ on earth, the Church universal, and is a Christian denomination in permanent mission to the unconverted, called into and sustained in being by God.

4. Denominational diversity is not self-evidently contrary to God's will for his people.

5. Inter-denominational harmony and co-operation are to be actively pursued for they are valuable for the enriching of the life and witness of the Body of Christ in the world and therefore of each denomination.

6. The Salvation Army welcomes involvement with other Christians in the many lands where the Army is privileged to witness and serve.

AMPLIFIED STATEMENT

The Body of Christ on Earth

1. *WE BELIEVE* that the Church, the Body of Christ on earth, often referred to in the New Testament as 'the saints' (*hoi hagioi* – Ephesians 1:23), comprises all who are born not of natural descent, nor of human decision, or a husband's will, but born of God (John 1:13). The Church universal includes all who believe in the Lord Jesus Christ, confessing him as Saviour and Lord, and witnessing to that sacred commitment through loving mutual submission (Matthew 18:15-20; John 13:34-35; Ephesians 5:21) and sacrificial service (Mark 8:34; Matthew 20:25-28; John 13:1-17).

   WE DO NOT BELIEVE that the Church universal depends for its existence or validity upon any particular ecclesiastical structure, any particular form of worship, or any particular observance of ritual.

2. *WE BELIEVE* that the Church universal is the whole of the worshipping, witnessing Christian community throughout the centuries

comprised of whatever groupings, large or small, accepted or persecuted, wealthy or poor, into which her members may have been gathered in the past or in the present.

WE DO NOT BELIEVE that an adequate definition of the Body of Christ on earth, the Church universal, can be confined in terms of ecclesiastical structure, but must rather be stated in terms of a spiritual relationship of grace that must find expression in all ecclesiastical structures. Members of the Body are those who are incorporate in Christ Jesus (Ephesians 1:1) and therefore reconciled to God through his Son. All such are in a spiritual relationship one with the other, which begins and continues regardless of externals, according to the prayer of Jesus that those who are his may be one (John 17:23). These words of Jesus ask for a oneness as is found in the oneness of Father, Son and Holy Spirit. This oneness is spiritual, not organizational.

3. *WE BELIEVE* that The Salvation Army belongs to, and is a particular communion of, the Church universal and a representative of the Body of Christ. Christ is the True Vine (John 15:1) and all believers are his living, fruit-bearing branches, exhorted by Scripture to live in Christlike unity (1 Corinthians 12:12).

WE DO NOT BELIEVE that any community made up of true followers of Christ can rightly be regarded as outside the Church universal, whatever their history, customs or practices when compared with those of other Christian communities. God alone knows those who are truly his (2 Timothy 2:19).

Denominational Variety

4. *WE BELIEVE* that God's dealings with his people are perfect according to his will, but that human responses are imperfect and prone to error. It may be God's dealings or fallible human responses to those dealings which have brought about the rich and varied denominational tapestry discernible today.

   WE DO NOT BELIEVE that denominational or organizational variety can automatically and in every case be said to be contrary to God's will for his people.

5. *WE BELIEVE* that God raised up The Salvation Army according to his purposes for his glory and for the proclamation and demonstration of the gospel.

   WE DO NOT BELIEVE that The Salvation Army's existence as an independent and distinctive Christian church, having no formal, structural ties with other Christian churches, is an affront to the gospel of Jesus Christ or self-evidently contrary to God's will for the whole of his Body on earth.

6. *WE BELIEVE* that the practices of The Salvation Army have much in common with the practices of other churches, but that being raised up by God for a distinctive work, the Army has been led of God to adopt the following combination of characteristics:

a) its emphasis upon personal religion and individual spiritual regeneration through faith in Christ leading in turn to a commitment in mission to seek to win others to Christ;

b) its commitment to the unceasing proclamation of the gospel and its insistence that this gospel is for the whosoever;

c) its teaching concerning sanctification and holy living;

d) its teaching that the receiving of inward spiritual grace is not dependent upon any particular outward observance;

e) its worldwide tradition of service (arising out of the compassionate love of Christ for all persons) without discrimination or preconditions, to the distressed, needy and marginalised, together with appropriate advocacy in the public domain on matters of social justice;

f) its willingness to obey the 'great commission' of Jesus Christ, under the guidance of the Holy Spirit, by ongoing expansion of Salvationist witness and service into new countries, with a consequential celebration, with thanksgiving to God, of its internationalism;

g) its preference for non-liturgical and flexible forms of worship, seeking to encourage spontaneity, for example in prayer and in spoken personal witness and testimony;

h) its tradition of inviting public response to the presentation of the gospel message, and its use of the mercy seat for this and other spiritual purposes;

i) its focus, in self-expression, on the biblical military metaphor of living in the world and of serving God as soldiers of Jesus Christ (2 Timothy 2:3; Ephesians 6:11-17);

j) its requirement that adults and children wishing to become full members (soldiers and junior soldiers), and thereby wishing to make a commitment to formal membership of the Body of Christ on earth, should publicly confess their faith in Jesus Christ as Saviour and Lord, the children making a simple statement of faith with promises as to lifestyle and the primary spiritual disciplines (see page 19), and the adults entering into formal doctrinal and ethical commitments, the latter focusing on the sacredness of human relationships, but including also the personal disciplines of abstention from alcohol, tobacco, and non-medical use of addictive drugs (see page 21);

k) its wearing of distinctive uniforms as a witness to belonging to Christ and as a signal of availability to others;

l) its encouragement into Salvation Army fellowship of those who do not wish to enter into the full commitment of soldiership (see j above), but are willing to become adherent members as a step in the journey of faith;

m) its recognition of the equal place within the Body of Christ of men and women in

8

all aspects of Christian service, ministry and leadership including the holding of ecclesiological authority;

n) its readiness to use all forms of musical expression in worship and evangelism, and its encouragement in many cultures of the indigenisation of worship expressions and styles.

WE DO NOT BELIEVE it to be self-evidently God's will for his people in the Army that they cast aside in haste the leadings of God or the blessings of the years, but rather, in humility, to value them, learn from them, and harness and adapt them for ongoing relevance in future witness and service.

The Local Church

7. *WE BELIEVE* that just as the true Church universal comprises all who believe on the Lord Jesus Christ, so each denominational church comprises a community of believers who have in common the way the Lord, through the Holy Spirit, has dealt with them as a community. In turn, each denominational church comprises local congregations regularly meeting together for worship, fellowship and service in a relatively confined geographical location.

WE DO NOT BELIEVE that the validity of a denomination or its local congregations depends upon any particular ecclesiastical tradition, structure, hierarchy, form of worship, or ritual. Where even two or three gather in Christ's name there he is present (Matthew 18:20) with a presence no less real than that discerned in larger, more formal, ceremonial or liturgical settings.

The Army's Identity

8. *WE BELIEVE* that The Salvation Army is an international Christian church in permanent mission to the unconverted, and is an integral part of the Body of Christ like other Christian churches, and that the Army's local corps are local congregations like the local congregations of other Christian churches. The Army springs from the Methodist Revival and has remained unassimilated by any other denomination. Like other reformers before him, William Booth did not intentionally set out to found a new denomination. However, through the years Salvationism has moved on in its emerging self-perception, and in the perceptions of others, from being a para-church evangelistic revival movement (at first known as The Christian Mission) to being a Christian church with a

10

permanent mission to the unsaved and the marginalised. Salvationists remain comfortable in being known simply as 'the Army', or a 'mission', or a 'movement', or for certain purposes as a 'charity'. All of these descriptors can be used alongside 'church'. With this multi-faceted identity the Army is welcomed to, and takes its place at, the ecumenical table at local, national and international levels.

WE DO NOT BELIEVE that The Salvation Army's history, structures, practices or beliefs permit it to be understood as anything other than a distinct Christian denomination with a purpose to fulfil and a calling to discharge under God. Similarly, its local corps cannot properly be understood unless seen primarily as local church congregations meeting regularly by grace and in Christ's name for worship, fellowship and service. Typically a local Army congregation will offer an integrated and holistic ministry, with both spiritual and social service dimensions, to the local population. Commissioned officers (both men and women) of The Salvation Army are duly ordained Christian leaders and ministers of the Christian gospel, called by God and empowered by the Holy Spirit to preach and teach biblical, apostolic truth (Acts 2:42), and to serve others in the name of Christ and for his sake.

The Army and Other Churches

9. *WE BELIEVE* that it is God's will that harmonious relations are built up and sustained, by divine grace, between Christians everywhere and between all Christian denominations including their local congregations. The Army's numerous and widespread contacts with other Christian communities around the world serve to enrich the Army and to enhance its understanding of the work of the Holy Spirit. For this reason the Army welcomes such contacts and seeks cordially to extend and deepen them.

   WE DO NOT BELIEVE that narrowness or exclusiveness are consistent with God's will for his people, or that God has nothing to teach us by our sharing and co-operating with his people in other denominations. As in humility we learn from others, also we come to the ecumenical table ready to share whatever God in his wisdom has graciously bestowed upon the Army.

10. *WE BELIEVE* that every visible expression of the Church universal is endowed with its own blessings and strengths as gifts from God. We respect and admire those strengths, recognising too that because of human frailty every such

expression, including The Salvation Army, has its imperfections.

WE DO NOT BELIEVE it is our task to comment negatively upon, or to undermine, the traditions of other denominations, and certainly not in relation to the sacraments (on which our distinctive, though not unique, position sees the whole of life as a sacrament with a calling from God to Salvationists to witness to a life of sanctity without formal sacraments). It is contrary to our practices to offer adverse comment upon the life of any denomination or local congregation. We seek to be careful not to belittle the doctrines or practices of any other Christian group. The Army places emphasis in its teaching not upon externals but upon the need for each believer personally to experience that inward spiritual grace to which an external observance testifies. We maintain that no external observance can rightly be said to be essential to salvation or to the receiving of divine grace and that the biblical truth is that we can meet with God and receive his grace anywhere at any time through faith. We recognise that external observances such as baptism and eucharist are used in many denominations as a means of grace. We believe that our calling into sanctity without sacraments is not a contradiction of the ways of other churches, but is something beautiful for Christ, to be held in creative tension with the equally beautiful, but very different, practices of other denominations. In the overall economy of God there are no inherent contradictions, but there are creative paradoxes.

11. *WE BELIEVE* that The Salvation Army was called into being by the will of God, is sustained in being by God's grace, and is empowered for obedience by the Holy Spirit. Its overriding purpose as encapsulated in the name God has given us – The Salvation Army – is therefore to strive to lead men and women and boys and girls into saving faith in Jesus Christ, working tirelessly and for Christ's sake, to develop them in holy living, that they might better serve suffering humanity while remaining unpolluted by the world (James 1:26, 27).

WE DO NOT BELIEVE that we alone are called to these sacred and awesome tasks, and therefore we rejoice exceedingly because in other Christian churches we find co-workers for God.

NOTE:

For Salvationist acceptance of the historic Christian creeds (The Apostles' Creed, The Nicene Creed, The Athanasian Creed) see *Salvation Story – Salvationist Handbook of Doctrine* (The Salvation Army, London, 1998).

APPENDIX

THE SALVATION ARMY'S ARTICLES OF FAITH

We believe that the Scriptures of the Old and New Testaments were given by inspiration of God, and that they only constitute the Divine rule of Christian faith and practice.

We believe that there is only one God, who is infinitely perfect, the Creator, Preserver, and Governor of all things, and who is the only proper object of religious worship.

We believe that there are three persons in the Godhead – the Father, the Son, and the Holy Ghost, undivided in essence and co-equal in power and glory.

We believe that in the person of Jesus Christ the Divine and human natures are united, so that he is truly and properly God and truly and properly man.

We believe that our first parents were created in a state of innocency, but by their disobedience, they lost their purity and happiness, and that in consequence of their fall, all men have become sinners, totally depraved, and as such are justly exposed to the wrath of God.

We believe that the Lord Jesus Christ has by his suffering and death made an atonement for the whole world so that whosoever will may be saved.

We believe that repentance toward God, faith in our Lord Jesus Christ and regeneration by the Holy Spirit are necessary to salvation.

We believe that we are justified by grace through faith in our Lord Jesus Christ and that he that believeth hath the witness in himself.

We believe that continuance in a state of salvation depends upon continued obedient faith in Christ.

We believe that it is the privilege of all believers to be wholly sanctified, and that their whole spirit and soul and body may be preserved blameless unto the coming of our Lord Jesus Christ.

We believe in the immortality of the soul, the resurrection of the body, in the general judgment at the end of the world, in the eternal happiness of the righteous, and in the endless punishment of the wicked.

JUNIOR SOLDIER'S PROMISE

Having asked God for forgiveness, I will be his loving and obedient child. Because Jesus is my Saviour from sin, I will trust him to keep me good, and will try to help others to follow him. I promise to pray, to read my Bible and, by his help, to lead a life that is clean in thought, word and deed. I will not smoke, take harmful drugs or drink alcoholic drinks.

SOLDIER'S COVENANT

Promises made when becoming a soldier in
The Salvation Army

HAVING accepted Jesus Christ as my Saviour and Lord, and desiring to fulfil my membership of his Church on earth as a soldier of The Salvation Army, I now by God's grace enter into a sacred covenant.

I believe and will live by the truths of the word of God expressed in The Salvation Army's eleven articles of faith:

We believe that the Scriptures of the Old and New Testaments were given by inspiration of God: and that they only constitute the Divine rule of Christian faith and practice.

We believe that there is only one God, who is infinitely perfect, the Creator. Preserver, and Governor of all things, and who is the only proper object of religious worship.

We believe that there are three persons in the Godhead – the Father, the Son and the Holy Ghost, undivided in essence and co-equal in power and glory.

We believe that in the person of Jesus Christ the Divine and human natures are united, so that he is truly and properly God and truly and properly man.

We believe that our first parents were created in a state of innocency, but by their disobedience they lost their purity and happiness; and that in consequence of their fall all men have become sinners, totally depraved. and as such are justly exposed to the wrath of God.

We believe that the Lord Jesus Christ has, by his suffering and death, made an atonement for the whole world so that whosoever will may be saved.

We believe that repentance towards God, faith in our Lord Jesus Christ and regeneration by the Holy Spirit are necessary to salvation.

We believe that we are justified by grace, through faith in our Lord Jesus Christ; and that he that believeth hath the witness in himself.

We believe that continuance in a state of salvation depends upon continued obedient faith in Christ.

We believe that it is the privilege of all believers to be wholly sanctified, and that their whole spirit and soul and body may be preserved blameless unto the coming of our Lord Jesus Christ.

We believe in the immortality of the soul; in the resurrection of the body; in the general judgment at the end of the world; in the eternal happiness of the righteous; and in the endless punishment of the wicked.

THEREFORE

I will be responsive to the Holy Spirit's work and obedient to his leading in my life, growing in grace through worship, prayer, service and the reading of the Bible.

I will make the values of the Kingdom of God and not the values of the world the standard for my life.

I will uphold Christian integrity in every area of my life, allowing nothing in thought, word or deed that is unworthy, unclean, untrue, profane, dishonest or immoral.

I will maintain Christian ideals in all my relationships with others: my family and neighbours, my colleagues and fellow Salvationists, those to whom and for whom I am responsible, and the wider community.

I will uphold the sanctity of marriage and of family life.

I will be a faithful steward of my time and gifts, my money and possessions, my body, my mind and my spirit, knowing that I am accountable to God.

I will abstain from alcoholic drink, tobacco, the non-medical use of addictive drugs, gambling, pornography, the occult, and all else that could enslave the body or spirit.

I will be faithful to the purposes for which God raised up The Salvation Army, sharing the good news of Jesus Christ, endeavouring to win others to him, and in his name caring for the needy and the disadvantaged.

I will be actively involved, as l am able, in the life, work, worship and witness of the corps, giving as large a proportion of my income as possible to support its ministries and the worldwide work of the Army.

I will be true to the principles and practices of The Salvation Army, loyal to its leaders, and I will show the spirit of Salvationism whether in times of popularity or persecution.

I now call upon all present to witness that I enter into this covenant and sign these articles of war of my own free will, convinced that the love of Christ, who died and now lives to save me, requires from me this devotion of my life to his service for the salvation of the whole world; and therefore do here declare my full determination, by God's help, to be a true soldier of The Salvation Army.

OFFICER'S COVENANT

MY COVENANT

Called by God to proclaim the gospel of our Lord and Saviour Jesus Christ as an officer of The Salvation Army, I bind myself to him in this solemn covenant: to love and serve him supremely all my days, to live to win souls and make their salvation the first purpose of my life, to care for the poor, feed the hungry, clothe the naked, love the unlovable, and befriend those who have no friends, to maintain the doctrines and principles of The Salvation Army, and, by God's grace, to prove myself a worthy officer.

Done in the strength of my Lord and Saviour, and in the presence of *[the following wording to be adapted to local circumstances]* the Territorial Commander, training college officers and fellow cadets.

L'ARMEE DU SALUT DANS
LE CORPS DE CHRIST

UNE DECLARATION ECCLESIOLOGIQUE

Déclaration provenant du Quartier Général International de l'Armée du Salut, et publiée avec l'autorité du Général, en consultation avec le Conseil International de Doctrine et le Conseil International de Management

L'ARMEE DU SALUT DANS LE CORPS DE CHRIST

Une Déclaration Ecclésiologique

Préface

C'est mon plaisir et mon privilège de faire parvenir aux salutistes du monde entier cette déclaration qui précise la place qu'occupe l'Armée du Salut au sein du Corps de Christ. Ce texte a passé par plusieurs étapes dans sa formulation et j'exprime ma profonde gratitude à tous ceux qui s'y sont investis, à commencer par le Conseil international de la Doctrine que préside le commissaire William Francis, aux membres du Conseil international de Management au Quartier Général International de Londres. Les délégués de ces deux corps constitués, de par leur composition multiethnique, apportent à la Déclaration leur universalité de regards et d'attitudes.

Nous avons désiré que cette déclaration serve à tous les salutistes pour qu'ils sachent et comprennent où se situe notre Armée parmi tant d'Eglises, de dénominations, de communautés para ecclésiales, synodes ou autres groupes de chrétiens autour du monde. Ce texte sera surtout utile à tous ceux et celles que leur tâche conduit dans les rencontres œcuméniques. De même, si nécessaire, cette déclaration pourra éclairer toute personne extérieure à nos rangs en vue de plus de compréhension mutuelle. Celle-ci n'a pas pour but de dire quelque chose de neuf, mais d'affirmer et de clarifier notre identité au sein du Corps de Christ, au vu de ce que le monde extérieur pense de nous.

Que Dieu bénisse et se serve de cette courte publication pour sa plus grande gloire, et que notre Armée reste prête et obéissante à suivre ses directives, demeurant une mission permanente auprès des les non convertis; une expression moderne, et même unique, de la vie de l'Eglise.

Shaw Clifton
Général
Avril 2008

SOMMAIRE DE LA DECLARATION

1. Le Corps de Christ sur la terre (également décrit dans ce document comme l'Eglise universelle) comprend l'ensemble de ceux qui croient en Jésus-Christ, Sauveur et Seigneur.

2. Ces croyants sont unis les uns aux autres dans une relation spirituelle indépendante de toute structure ecclésiastique particulière.

3. L'Armée du Salut, soumise et appartenant au seul Dieu - un en trois personnes - est une expression du Corps de Christ ici-bas, l'Eglise universelle; elle est une dénomination chrétienne en mission permanente envers les les non convertis, suscitée et préservée par Dieu.

4. La diversité des dénominations n'est pas nécessairement un fait contraire à la volonté de Dieu.

5. L'harmonie et la coopération inter ecclésiastiques sont à rechercher activement pour l'enrichissement de la vie et du témoignage du Corps de Christ dans le monde, enrichissement donc de chaque dénomination.

6. L'Armée du Salut voit d'une manière positive tout engagement et collaboration avec d'autres chrétiens, dans tout pays où elle aurait le privilège de témoigner et de servir.

DÉCLARATION GENERALE

Le Corps de Christ sur la terre

1. **NOUS CROYONS** que L'Eglise, Corps de Christ sur la terre, souvent décrite dans le Nouveau Testament par l'expression 'les saints' (*hoi hagioi* -Ephésiens 1:23) comprend quiconque est né, non d'une descendance physique ou du vouloir humain, mais qui est né de Dieu (Jean 1:13). L'Eglise universelle englobe quiconque croit au Seigneur Jésus-Christ, le confesse comme Sauveur et Seigneur, témoigne d'un engagement sacré que traduisent une soumission mutuelle (Matthieu 18:15-20; Jean 13:34, 35; Ephésiens 5:21) et un service empreint du don de soi (Marc 8:34; Matthieu 20:25-28; Jean 13: 1-17).

   MAIS NOUS NE CROYONS PAS que l'Eglise universelle fonde son existence et sa validité sur quelque structure ecclésiastique, sur quelque forme de culte particulière ou sur quelque observance d'un rite.

2. **NOUS CROYONS** que l'Eglise universelle est constituée par l'ensemble des familles

chrétiennes qui servent et confessent Jésus-Christ et ce, au travers de l'histoire: communautés riches ou pauvres, acceptées ou persécutées, nombreuses ou non, au sein desquelles ses membres ont été accueillis dans le passé ou le présent.

MAIS NOUS NE CROYONS PAS qu'une définition adéquate du Corps de Christ sur la terre, l'Eglise universelle, puisse être confinée en termes de structure de type ecclésiastique. Cette définition doit plutôt refléter une relation spirituelle fondée sur la grâce, relation qui doit apparaître dans n'importe quelle structure ecclésiastique. Les membres de ce Corps sont ceux qui ont été greffés au Christ Jésus (Ephésiens 1:1) et par conséquent réconciliés avec Dieu par son Fils. Les membres ainsi définis sont aussi liés les uns aux autres par une relation spirituelle qui se bâtit et se maintient quelle que soit l'apparence, et selon la prière de Jésus 'que ceux qui lui appartiennent soient un' (Jean 17:23). Là, Jésus intercède pour une unité semblable à celle qui unit le Père, le Fils et le Saint-Esprit. Une telle unité est d'ordre spirituel et non organisationnel.

3. **NOUS CROYONS** que l'Armée du Salut, en tant que communion particulière de fidèles, appartient à l'Eglise universelle et se veut une

représentante du Corps de Christ. Christ est le vrai cep (Jean 15:1); chaque croyant est son sarment, vivant, fécond, appelé par l'Ecriture à vivre l'unité puisée dans la nature même de Christ.

MAIS NOUS NE CROYONS PAS qu'une communauté composée de vrais disciples du Christ puisse être considérée comme étrangère à l'Eglise universelle quelle que soit son histoire, ses coutumes ou ses pratiques comparées à celles d'autres communautés chrétiennes car 'Dieu lui seul reconnaît les siens'. (2 Timothée 2:19).

Variétés de dénominations

4. **NOUS CROYONS** que la manière d'agir de Dieu envers son peuple est parfaite, et reflète sa volonté mais que les réponses humaines sont imparfaites et sujettes à erreur. Qu'il vienne de Dieu, ou des réactions faillibles des hommes à ses intentions, le résultat a produit la trame si riche et si variée de toutes les dénominations existant actuellement.

MAIS NOUS NE CROYONS PAS que la variété de dénominations et d'organisations soit toujours et automatiquement contraire à la volonté de Dieu.

5. **NOUS CROYONS** que Dieu a suscité l'Armée du Salut selon ses desseins, pour sa plus grande gloire, et pour la proclamation et la démonstration de l'Evangile.

MAIS NOUS NE CROYONS PAS que l'existence de l'Armée du Salut comme Eglise chrétienne indépendante et distincte - sans liens formels ou structurels avec d'autres Eglises chrétiennes - soit une offense à l'Evangile de Jésus-Christ ou nécessairement contraire à sa volonté pour l'ensemble de son corps ici-bas.

6. **NOUS CROYONS** que les méthodes de l'Armée du Salut ont quantité de similitudes avec celles d'autres Eglises, à la différence que celle-ci fut créée par Dieu en vue d'une tâche distincte. A cet effet, Dieu l'a conduite à adopter les caractéristiques suivantes:

a) l'accent mis sur une religion personnelle et sur la régénération spirituelle, par la foi en Christ, qui engendre un engagement missionnaire en vue de chercher et gagner quiconque pour Christ;

b) son engagement à une incessante proclamation de l'Evangile et son insistance pour qu'il s'adresse à tous;

c) son enseignement de la sanctification et de la vie sainte;

d) son enseignement que la jouissance d'une grâce spirituelle intérieure ne dépend d'aucune observance extérieure particulière;

e) sa tradition de service mondialement démontrée (fruit de l'amour et de la compassion de Christ pour toute personne) sans discrimination, sans condition, vers toute détresse, vers chaque besoin, vers chaque marginal, accompagnée de tout support approprié venant du domaine public en matière de justice sociale;

f) son obéissance volontaire à l'appel divin de Jésus-Christ et sous la direction du Saint-Esprit, son engagement en vue de l'expansion continue du service et du témoignage salutistes vers de nouveaux horizons, débouchant sur des célébrations consécutives à son internationalisme avec des actions de grâce;

g) sa préférence marquée pour des formes de culte flexibles, non liturgiques, encourageant la spontanéité dans la prière et dans le témoignage personnel exprimés en public;

h) sa tradition d'encourager une réponse publique à la proclamation de l'Evangile par l'emploi du Banc de la repentance, pour ceci ou pour quelque autre démarche spirituelle;

i) sa manière d'illustrer corporellement la métaphore biblique militaire: 'de vivre dans ce monde, et de servir Dieu comme des soldats de Jésus-Christ' (2 Timothée 2:3; Ephésiens 6:11-17);

j) sa requête instante afin que tout adulte ou enfant, souhaitant devenir membre à part entière (soldat senior ou junior), et désirant pour cela signer un engagement formel de membre du Corps de Christ ici-bas, confesse sa foi en Jésus-Christ son Sauveur et Seigneur: l'enfant faisant une simple déclaration de foi avec promesses d'un style de vie simple et d'une discipline spirituelle adaptée (voir page 19), l'adulte acceptant une base doctrinale et un engagement éthique, démarche qui souligne le caractère sacré de toute relation humaine, complétée en plus par cette discipline personnelle: abstention d'alcool, de tabac, et de toute consommation de drogue hors d'une prescription médicale (voir page 21);

k) le port d'un uniforme distinctif comme témoignage d'appartenance à Christ, et comme signe de disponibilité envers tous;

l) l'encouragement à rejoindre la communauté salutiste à quiconque ne souhaite pas entrer dans un engagement complet comme soldat (voir ci-dessus lettre j) mais qui considère que devenir membre adhérent est comme une étape de son itinéraire spirituel;

m) d'insister, au sein du Corps de Christ, sur l'égalité entre hommes et femmes et sur l'équivalence entre serviteurs et servantes dans tous les aspects d'un service chrétien: exercice d'un ministère ou d'une responsabilité quelle qu'elle soit, y compris le mandat d'une autorité ecclésiastique;

n) sa disposition à employer toutes les expressions musicales possibles dans le culte et l'évangélisation, pour encourager où que ce soit et quelle que soit la culture locale, l'adaptation aux styles et aux formes de culte.

MAIS NOUS NE CROYONS PAS que Dieu voie volontiers son peuple faire peu de cas de son histoire et oublier trop vite les directions et les bénédictions divines de son passé. Au contraire! Qu'avec humilité il en discerne leur valeur, apprenne et profite de leurs leçons et les garde en mémoire, car les directions et bénédictions passées sont autant d'acquis en vue de son témoignage et de son service à venir.

L'Eglise locale

7. **NOUS CROYONS** que, tout comme la véritable Eglise universelle englobe quiconque croit au Seigneur Jésus-Christ, ainsi toute Eglise confessionnelle, formée d'une communauté de croyants par l'action du Saint-Esprit, peut témoigner des interventions du Seigneur en sa faveur. A leur tour, ces Eglises confessionnelles se composent de congrégations locales, celles-ci se retrouvant régulièrement pour le culte, la vie communautaire et le service, dans une région géographique distincte.

MAIS NOUS NE CROYONS PAS que la validité d'une telle dénomination ou de ses congrégations locales dépende d'une tradition ecclésiale quelconque, de sa structure, de sa hiérarchie, de ses formes cultuelles ou de ses rites. Là où deux ou trois s'assemblent au nom du Christ, il est présent (Matthieu 18:20), présence non moins évidente que celle ressentie dans des assemblées plus grandes, plus formelles, plus solennelles de par leur contenu liturgique.

Notre identité salutiste

8. **NOUS CROYONS** que l'Armée du Salut est une Eglise chrétienne internationale engagée en permanence dans la mission en faveur des non convertis; elle est une partie intégrante du Corps de Christ comme toute Eglise chrétienne, et la congrégation du Poste salutiste local est en tout point semblable aux congrégations d'autres Eglises chrétiennes. L'Armée est issue du Réveil méthodiste tout en restant indépendante et distincte de toute autre dénomination. Semblable à d'autres réformateurs qui l'ont précédé, William Booth n'avait pas l'intention de fonder une nouvelle communauté. Mais au travers des âges, le salutisme s'est forgé sa propre image, image également perçue par d'autres, comme un mouvement de réveil para ecclésiastique (connu au départ sous le nom de Mission chrétienne) pour devenir une Eglise chrétienne en mission permanente envers les les non convertis et les marginaux. Les salutistes se sentent à l'aise quand on les décrit comme 'Armée', 'Mission', ou 'Mouvement' et dans certains cas, 'Œuvre de charité'. Tous ces qualificatifs peuvent s'accoler au terme 'église'. Avec cette identité à multiples facettes, l'Armée est accueillie et prend sa place à la table œcuménique au niveau local, national, ou international.

MAIS NOUS NE CROYONS PAS que l'Armée du Salut dans son histoire, sa structure ses méthodes et son credo, puisse être regardée autrement qu'une dénomination chrétienne distincte, avec un objectif à atteindre, et une mission dont elle répond devant Dieu. De même, un Poste local ne sera pas considéré autrement qu'une congrégation chrétienne vivant de la grâce et se rencontrant au nom du Christ pour le culte offert à Dieu dans la communion et le service. Cette congrégation salutiste locale offrira un ministère holistique intégral, comprenant des activités de type spirituel ou social au profit de la population locale. Ses officiers consacrés (hommes et femmes) sont dûment ordonnés comme responsables chrétiens et ministres de l'Evangile de Christ, oints et remplis du Saint-Esprit pour prêcher et enseigner toute vérité biblique apostolique (Actes 2:42) et pour servir leurs contemporains au nom du Christ, remplis de son amour.

L'Armée du Salut et les autres Eglises

9. **NOUS CROYONS** qu'il est dans la volonté de Dieu et que c'est un effet de sa grâce, que des relations harmonieuses naissent et subsistent entre les chrétiens où qu'ils soient, entre toutes

les dénominations chrétiennes et leurs congrégations locales pareillement. L'Armée du Salut, de par ses nombreux contacts avec d'autres Eglises, et son ouverture au niveau international s'en enrichit elle-même et découvre toujours plus comment agit le Saint-Esprit. Pour cette raison, l'Armée recherche ardemment ces contacts, les augmente et les approfondit.

MAIS NOUS NE CROYONS PAS que l'étroitesse d'esprit ou quelque attitude exclusive soient consistantes face à la volonté de Dieu pour son peuple, ni que Dieu n'ait rien à nous apprendre hors des partages et des collaborations avec son peuple vivant dans d'autres dénominations. Dans l'humilité, nous apprenons d'elles, dans la fraternité nous prenons place à la table œcuménique, toujours disposés à partager ce que Dieu dans sa sagesse a généreusement donné à l'Armée.

10. **NOUS CROYONS** que toutes les expressions visibles de l'Eglise universelle ont été abondamment dotées de bénédictions propres et de capacité d'agir, autant de dons de Dieu. Nous respectons et admirons ces forces admettant que, dues aux fragilités humaines, toutes ces expressions, y compris notre Armée, a ses imperfections.

MAIS NOUS NE CROYONS PAS avoir le droit de commenter négativement, voire de miner les traditions d'autres dénominations et certainement pas au sujet des sacrements (sur lesquels notre position distinctive, mais non unique, considère toute notre vie comme un sacrement avec un appel de Dieu aux salutistes de témoigner d'une vie sainte sans l'aide de formes sacramentelles). Il est contraire à nos principes d'exprimer quelque commentaire à l'encontre de la vie d'une dénomination ou congrégation locale. Nous avons soin de ne jamais déprécier les doctrines et les pratiques d'autres groupes chrétiens. L'enseignement de l'Armée, loin de souligner l'aspect extérieur de la foi, met l'accent sur la nécessité pour chaque croyant d'expérimenter la grâce spirituelle intérieure, expérience indépendante de toute observance rituelle. Cet enseignement dit notre conviction qu'aucune pratique extérieure n'est nécessaire au salut ou à la bénédiction de la grâce divine, expériences fondées sur la vérité biblique: à savoir que nous avons par la foi accès à la présence et Dieu et à sa grâce à tout instant et où que nous soyons. Nous reconnaissons que des rites comme le baptême et l'eucharistie, sont reconnus dans nombre de dénominations comme moyens de grâce. Nous croyons que notre appel à la sainteté sans la pratique des sacrements, n'est nullement en contradiction avec les rites d'autres Eglises. Notre pratique a sa propre beauté dans le service pour Christ, de même que les pratiques différentes d'autres communautés ont leur beauté particulière. Dans l'économie divine du reste, il n'existe pas de contradiction propre; il n'y a qu'un esprit créatif qui transcende tout paradoxe.

11. **NOUS CROYONS** que l'Armée du Salut est née par la volonté de Dieu. Elle est maintenue par sa grâce et trouve sa force dans l'obéissance au Saint-Esprit. Son objectif suprême, inscrit dans le nom qui lui a été donné 'Armée du Salut' implique un combat: conduire hommes et femmes, garçons et filles à la foi en Jésus-Christ; rappeler qu'il faut travailler sans relâche et pour l'amour de son Nom, à développer chez tous la sainteté de vie, afin de toujours mieux servir l'humanité souffrante, tout en se gardant des impuretés du monde (Jacques 1:26, 27).

MAIS NOUS NE CROYONS PAS être les seuls appelés à cette tâche sacrée et admirable! Par conséquent notre joie est grande de voir d'autres Eglises chrétiennes en action et d'y trouver maints collaborateurs dans l'œuvre de Dieu.

NOTE:

Ouvrages et textes accessibles aux salutistes : tout credo historique (Nicée, Symbole des Apôtres, credo d'Athanase) et le *Manuel de Doctrines.*

ENGAGEMENT DE JEUNNE SOLDAT

Je crois que Dieu m'aime, pardonne mes péchés et me gardera toujours. Je veux aimer Jésus-Christ, mon Sauveur, et Lui confier ma vie. Je veux prier et lire ma Bible régulièrement, et aider mes semblables à trouver le Seigneur. Je veux être pur en pensées, en paroles et en actes. Je refuserai l'alcool, le tabac et la drogue, ainsi que tout produit qui entraîne une dépendance et nuit à ma santé. Avec l'aide de Dieu, je promets d'être un fidèle jeune soldat.

ENGAGEMENT DE SOLDAT

Articles de Guerre

Ayant accepté Jésus-Christ pour mon Sauveur et Seigneur, et désirant faire partie de son Eglise sur terre comme soldat de l'Armée du Salut, je prends aujourd'hui, par la grâce de Dieu, un engagement sacré. Je crois aux vérités de la Parole de Dieu auxquelles je conformerai ma vie et que l'Armée du Salut formule ainsi dans ses onze articles de foi:

Nous croyons que les Ecritures de l'Ancien et du Nouveau Testament ont été données par l'inspiration de Dieu, et qu'elles seules constituent la règle divine de la foi et de la vie chrétiennes.

Nous croyons qu'il y a un seul Dieu, infiniment parfait, Créateur, Conservateur et Gouverneur de toutes choses – unique objet digne de l'adoration religieuse.

Nous croyons qu'il y a dans ce Dieu unique, trois personnes réellement distinctes, mais égales en puissance et en gloire: le Père, le Fils et le Saint-Esprit.

Nous croyons que dans la personne de Jésus-Christ la nature divine est unie à la nature humaine, de sorte que Jésus-Christ est véritablement Dieu et véritablement homme.

Nous croyons que nos premiers parents furent créés en état d'innocence, mais que, par leur désobéissance, ils perdirent leur pureté primitive et le bonheur. En conséquence de la chute, tous les hommes sont devenus pécheurs, entièrement mauvais, et pour cette raison, ils sont à bon droit exposés à la colère de Dieu.

Nous croyons que notre Seigneur Jésus-Christ, par ses souffrances et sa mort, a réconcilié le monde entier avec Dieu; ainsi quiconque le veut, peut être sauvé.

Nous croyons que la repentance envers Dieu, la foi en notre Seigneur Jésus-Christ, et la régénération par le Saint-Esprit sont nécessaires au salut.

Nous croyons que c'est par grâce que nous sommes justifiés, par la foi en notre Seigneur Jésus-Christ, et que celui qui croit en a le témoignage en lui-même.

Nous croyons que la possession permanente du salut dépend de la foi constante en Christ et de l'obéissance à sa parole.

Nous croyons que c'est le privilège de tous les enfants de Dieu d'être sanctifiés tout entiers, et que tout leur être, l'esprit, l'âme et le corps, peut être conservé irrépréhensible pour l'avènement de notre Seigneur Jésus-Christ (1 Th 5: 23).

Nous croyons à l'immortalité de l'âme, à la résurrection du corps, au jugement universel lors de la fin du monde, au bonheur éternel des justes et au châtiment éternel des méchants.

Je serai docile à l'action du Saint-Esprit et sensible à son intervention dans la conduite de ma vie, croissant dans la grâce par la participation aux cultes, la pratique de la prière, la lecture de la Bible et le service.

Je prendrai pour normes de ma vie les valeurs propres au Royaume de Dieu et non celles du monde.

Je respecterai l'intégrité chrétienne dan tous les aspects de ma vie, ne me permettant rien en pensées, paroles ou actes, qui soit méprisable ou impur, faux ou profane, malhonnête ou immoral.

Je maintiendrai l'idéal chrétien dans tous mes rapports avec autrui, ma famille, mes voisins, mes collègues et mes camarades salutistes, avec toute personne envers qui et de qui je suis responsable, et avec mes semblables en général.

Je respecterai le caractère sacré du mariage et de la vie de famille.

J'agirai comme un gestionnaire fidèle de mon temps et de mes dons, de mon argent et de mes biens, de mon corps, de mon âme et de mon esprit, sachant que j'en suis responsable envers Dieu.

Je m'abstiendrai des boissons alcooliques, du tabac, de la drogue non prescrits médicalement, des jeux de hasard, da la pornographie, de l'occultisme et de toute autre chose susceptible d'asservir le corps ou l'esprit.

Je poursuivrai loyalement les buts pour lesquels Dieu a suscité l'Armée du Salut, faisant connaître la Bonne Nouvelle de Jésus-Christ, m'efforçant de gagner d'autres personnes au Sauveur et en son nom, de soulager les nécessiteux et les défavorisés.

Dans la mesure de mes moyens, je m'associerai activement à la vie, au travail, au culte et au témoignage du poste, donnant, pour soutenir son ministère et l'œuvre de l'Armée dans le monde, une proportion de mes revenus aussi élevée que possible.

Je serai loyal envers les principes et les pratiques de l'Armée du Salut, loyal envers ses chefs, et je manifesterai l'esprit salutiste aussi bien au temps de la popularité qu'en période de persécution.

Je prends à témoin toutes les personnes ici présentes que je contracte cette alliance et signe ces Articles de Guerre de ma propre et libre volonté, sachant que l'amour du Christ, mort et ressuscité pour me sauver, réclame de moi cette consécratrion de ma vie à son service pour le salut du monde. En conséquence, je déclare ma pleine détermination d'être avec l'aide de Dieu, un vrai soldat de l'Armée du Salut.

ALLIANCE D'OFFICIER

Appelé par Dieu à proclamer l'évangile de notre Seigneur et Sauveur Jésus-Christ comme officier(ère) de l'Armée du Salut, Je conclus avec lui cette alliance solennelle:

Je veux l'aimer et le servir de tout mon cœur tous les jours de ma vie.

Je veux gagner les hommes à Christ; leur salut sera le but de ma vie.

Je prendrai soin des pauvres, je nourrirai les affamés, je vêtirai ceux qui sont nus, j'aimerai les mal-aimés et je sera l'ami des sans amis.

Je serai loyal envers les doctrines et les principes de l'Armée du Salut et, par la grâce de Dieu, je me comporterai d'une manière digne d'un officier et d'un disciple de Jésus-Christ.

EL EJÉRCITO DE SALVACIÓN EN EL CUERPO DE CRISTO

DECLARACIÓN ECLESIOLÓGICA

Declaración emitida por el Cuartel Internacional del Ejército de Salvación con la autorización del General y en consulta con el Consejo de Doctrina Internacional y el Consejo de Administración Internacional

EL EJÉRCITO DE SALVACIÓN EN EL CUERPO DE CRISTO

Declaración Eclesiológica

Prefacio

Me complace presentarles a los salvacionistas de todo el mundo la presente declaración acerca de la posición del Ejército de Salvación dentro del Cuerpo de Cristo. La misma ha atravesado múltiples etapas de preparación, por lo que quisiera expresar mi especial agradecimiento a todos aquellos que han contribuido con este proyecto, sin dejar de mencionar a los miembros del Consejo de Doctrina Internacional, encabezados por su Presidente, el Comisionado William Francis, así como a los miembros del Consejo de Administración Internacional del Cuartel Internacional de Londres. Estos dos Consejos, gracias a su composición multiétnica, representan actitudes y opiniones de la globalidad.

La presente declaración tiene como propósito ayudar a los salvacionistas a entender cuál es nuestra posición respecto a las diversas iglesias, denominaciones, cuerpos paraeclesiásticos, consejos eclesiásticos y demás grupos cristianos que existen en el mundo. La misma será de gran utilidad para aquellos que participen activamente en las actividades ecuménicas, quienes también podrán extenderlas a otras personas que no pertenezcan a nuestra organización con el ánimo de promover el entendimiento mutuo. El objetivo de la declaración no es señalar nuevas opiniones sino aclarar y consolidar la opinión global actual respecto a nuestra identidad dentro de todo el Cuerpo de Cristo.

Que Dios les bendiga y utilice esta breve publicación para su gloria eterna. Que el Ejército de Salvación esté siempre listo para obedecer su liderazgo, siendo en todo momento una misión permanente para los inconversos así como una expresión moderna y, hasta única, de la vida de la iglesia.

Shaw Clifton
General
Abril de 2008

RESUMEN DE LA DECLARACIÓN

1   El Cuerpo de Cristo en la tierra (al cual también nos referimos en la presente como 'la Iglesia universal') abarca a todos los creyentes en Jesucristo como Señor y Salvador.

2   Los creyentes establecen una relación espiritual mutua que no depende de ninguna estructura eclesiástica específica.

3   El Ejército de Salvación, bajo el Trino Dios, pertenece al Cuerpo de Cristo en la tierra - la Iglesia universal - y es parte del mismo. Asimismo, es una denominación cuya misión permanente es con los inconversos, llamada y sustentada por la gracia de Dios.

4   La diversidad denominacional no es intrínsicamente contraria a la voluntad de Dios para con su pueblo.

5   Deberán buscarse intensamente la armonía y la cooperación interdenominacionales ya que son

inestimables para el enriquecimiento de la vida y el testimonio del Cuerpo de Cristo en el mundo y, por tanto, inestimables para cada denominación.

6 El Ejército de Salvación acoge la participación de otros cristianos en los numerosos países en los que el Ejército tiene el privilegio de ofrecer su testimonio y su servicio.

DECLARACIÓN DETALLADA

El Cuerpo de Cristo en la tierra

1. CREEMOS que la Iglesia, el Cuerpo de Cristo en la tierra - al que el Nuevo Testamento a menudo se refiere como a 'los santos' (*hoi hagioi,* Efesios 1:23) - abarca a todos los que nacen no de la sangre, ni por decisiones naturales, ni por voluntad humana, sino los que nacen de Dios (Juan 1:13, *NVI*). La Iglesia universal incluye a todos los que creen en el Señor Jesús, lo confiesan como su Señor y Salvador y son testimonios de ese sagrado compromiso mediante el mutuo sometimiento con amor (Mateo 18:15-20; Juan 13:34-35; Efesios 5:21) y el servicio sacrificial (Marcos 8:34; Mateo 20:25-28; Juan 13:1-17).

    NO CREEMOS que la existencia o validez de la Iglesia universal dependa de ninguna estructura eclesiástica específica, de ninguna forma de adoración ni de la celebración de rituales específicos.

2. CREEMOS que la Iglesia universal está constituida por todo el conjunto de la

comunidad cristiana que ha adorado y testificado a través de los siglos, y que esta comunidad se compone de grupos grandes o pequeños, aceptados o perseguidos, ricos o pobres cuyos miembros se hayan reunido en el pasado o en el presente.

NO CREEMOS que la definición adecuada del Cuerpo de Cristo en la tierra —la Iglesia universal— pueda reducirse a nociones relativas de la estructura eclesiástica, sino que ha de ser explicada según la relación espiritual de la gracia que ha de revelarse en todas las estructuras eclesiásticas. Los miembros del Cuerpo son aquellos que se incorporan en Cristo Jesús (Efesios 1:1) y que de este modo se reconcilian con Dios a través de su Hijo. Estas personas establecen una relación espiritual mutua que tiene su origen y se desarrolla sin tener en cuenta los factores externos, siguiendo así la oración de Jesús de que los que son suyos, sean uno (Juan 17:23). Estas palabras de Jesús apuntan a la cohesión que se encuentra en la unidad del Padre, el Hijo y el Espíritu Santo. Esta unidad es espiritual, no organizacional.

3.   CREEMOS que el Ejército de Salvación pertenece y esta en comunión con la Iglesia universal, y representa al Cuerpo de Cristo. Cristo es la vid verdadera (Juan 15:1) y todos

los creyentes son ramas vivas que producen frutos y son exhortados por las Escrituras a vivir en unidad cristiana (1 Corintios 12:12).

NO CREEMOS que ninguna comunidad constituida por verdaderos seguidores de Cristo pueda ser considerada ajena a la Iglesia universal, sea cual fuere su historia, costumbres o prácticas al compararlas con las de otras comunidades cristianas. Sólo Dios conoce a los que verdaderamente son suyos (2 Timoteo 2:19).

Variedad denominacional

4. CREEMOS que las relaciones de Dios con su pueblo son perfectas según su voluntad, pero que las respuestas humanas son imperfectas y demuestran nuestra propensión al error. Las relaciones de Dios o las respuestas falibles de los seres humanos ante las mismas son las que quizás han generado el rico y variado tapiz denominacional que se puede apreciar hoy en día.

NO CREEMOS que se pueda afirmar automáticamente que cada uno de los casos de la variedad denominacional u organizacional sea contraria a la voluntad de Dios para su pueblo.

5. CREEMOS que Dios ha levantado el Ejército de Salvación según sus propósitos tanto para su gloria como para la proclamación y proclamación del Evangelio.

   NO CREEMOS que la existencia del Ejército de Salvación como Iglesia cristiana diferente y sin lazos formales ni estructurales con otras iglesias cristianas sea una afrenta al Evangelio de Jesucristo o sea evidentemente contraria a la voluntad de Dios para con todo su Cuerpo en la tierra.

6. CREEMOS que las prácticas del Ejército de Salvación son afines a las de otras iglesias, pero que habiendo sido levantado por Dios para una obra específica, Él le ha señalado la adopción de la siguiente combinación de características:

   a) el énfasis en la religión individual y la regeneración espiritual del individuo a través de su fe en Cristo de modo que lo conduzca a un compromiso con la misión de ganar almas para Cristo.

   b) el compromiso con la proclamación continua del Evangelio y el hincapié en el hecho de que el mismo es para todo aquel que quiera.

c) la enseñanza con respecto a la santificación y la vida santa.

d) la enseñanza de que la recepción de la gracia espiritual interior no depende de ninguna demostración exterior.

e) la tradición mundial de servicio (que emana del compasivo amor de Cristo para todas las personas) sin discriminación ni limitaciones a los afligidos, los necesitados y los marginados, a lo que se une la defensa de los asuntos relacionados con la justicia social en el dominio publico.

f) la disposición de obedecer la 'Gran Comisión' de Jesucristo bajo la guía del Espíritu Santo mediante la ampliación constante de los testimonios y servicios salvacionistas en nuevos países, seguida de la celebración y el agradecimiento a Dios por el internacionalismo alcanzado mediante dicha ampliación.

g) la preferencia por formas de adoración flexibles y desvinculadas de la liturgia con el fin de fomentar la espontaneidad, por ejemplo, en las oraciones y los testimonios personales pronunciados.

h) la tradición de invitar a responder públicamente ante la presentación del mensaje del Evangelio; el uso del Banco de Penitentes para este fin así como para otros fines espirituales.

i) el enfoque —que encuentra su expresión en el Ejército mismo— en la metáfora militar de vivir en el mundo y de servirle a Dios como soldados de Cristo Jesús (2 Timoteo 2:3; Efesios 6:11-17).

j) el requisito de que los adultos y los niños que aspiren ser miembros plenos (soldados y jóvenes soldados), y por ende, deseen comprometerse formalmente con el Cuerpo de Cristo en la tierra, deban confesar públicamente su fe en Jesucristo como Señor y Salvador; los niños hacen una sencilla declaración de fe con promesas relativas al estilo de vida y las disciplinas espirituales fundamentales, y los adultos establecen compromisos doctrinales y éticos, estos últimos con énfasis en la naturaleza sagrada de las relaciones humanas que incluye el acatamiento personal a la abstinencia al alcohol, al tabaco y al uso no facultativo de drogas.

k) el uso de uniformes específicos como testimonio de pertenencia a Cristo y señal de disponibilidad ante el prójimo.

l) la exhortación a la comunión con el Ejército de Salvación a aquellos que no desean comprometerse plenamente como soldados (véase inciso j) pero que están dispuestos a dar un paso adelante en la jornada de la fe y ser miembros adherentes.

m) el reconocimiento de la igualdad entre hombres y mujeres dentro del Cuerpo de Cristo en todos aspectos del servicio, el ministerio y el liderazgo cristiano, incluyendo el desempeño de la autoridad eclesiástica.

n) el interés manifiesto en la utilización de todo tipo de expresiones musicales para la adoración y el evangelismo así como la exhortación al empleo de los estilos y expresiones de adoración autóctonos de las diferentes culturas.

NO CREEMOS que sea voluntad de Dios para con su pueblo del Ejército que este eche a un lado precipitadamente la dirección divina o las bendiciones logradas con los años, sino que, con humildad, las valore, las estime, aprenda de ellas, y las encauce y adapte para darles una mayor relevancia en los testimonios y servicios futuros.

La Iglesia local

7. CREEMOS que así como la verdadera Iglesia universal abarca a todos aquellos que creen en el Señor Jesucristo, cada denominación eclesiástica abarca una comunidad de creyentes que comparten la manera en que el Señor, mediante el Espíritu Santo, se relaciona con ellos. A su vez, cada denominación eclesiástica se compone de congregaciones locales que se reúnen periódicamente para la adoración, la comunión y el servicio en una zona geográfica relativamente circunscrita.

NO CREEMOS que la validez de una denominación o de sus congregaciones locales dependa de ninguna tradición, estructura o jerarquía eclesiástica, forma de adoración o ritual específico. En cualquier lugar dónde se reúnan aunque sean dos o tres personas en el nombre de Cristo, Él estará en medio de ellos (Mateo 18:20) con una presencia tan real como la que se evidencia en ambientes más grandes, más formales, más ceremoniales o más litúrgicos.

La identidad del Ejército

8. CREEMOS que el Ejército de Salvación es una Iglesia cristiana internacional cuya misión permanente es con los inconversos, y que es parte integral del Cuerpo de Cristo al igual que lo son otras iglesias cristianas, y que los Cuerpos locales del Ejército son congregaciones iguales a las de otras iglesias cristianas. El Ejército nace producto del Avivamiento Metodista y nunca ha sido asimilado por ninguna otra denominación. Como otros reformadores anteriores a él, la intención de William Booth no era la de crear una nueva denominación. Sin embargo, con el transcurso del tiempo, el salvacionismo ha transformado su imagen fundacional y la percepción del público, y a partir de un movimiento evangelístico de avivamiento paraeclesiástico (conocido al principio como La Misión Cristiana) se ha convertido en una iglesia cristiana con una misión permanente entre los inconversos y los marginados. Los salvacionistas se sienten satisfechos con ser conocidos sencillamente como 'el Ejército', como una 'misión', como un 'movimiento', o para fines específicos, como una 'institución caritativa'. Todas estas descripciones se pueden añadir al nombre de 'iglesia'. Debido a esta identidad

multifacética, el Ejército recibe invitaciones y participa en las reuniones ecuménicas a instancias locales, nacionales e internacionales.

NO CREEMOS que la historia, las estructuras ni las prácticas o creencias del Ejército de Salvación apunten a una percepción del Ejército que no sea la de ser una denominación cristiana diferente cuyo propósito y llamado es el cumplimiento de la voluntad y la obra de Dios. De igual manera, no se podrá entender todo el significado de sus Cuerpos locales si no se les percibe como congregaciones de iglesias locales que se reúnen periódicamente por gracia divina y en el nombre de Cristo para la adoración, la comunión y el servicio. Normalmente, las congregaciones locales del Ejército ofrecen un ministerio integral y holístico, con una dimensión tanto espiritual como de servicio social a la población. Los oficiales comisionados del Ejército de Salvación (tanto hombres como mujeres) son líderes cristianos y ministros del Evangelio cristiano ordenados formalmente, llamados por Dios y capacitados por el Espíritu Santo para predicar y enseñar la verdad bíblica y apostólica (Hechos 2:42) y para servirle al prójimo en nombre de Cristo y para su gloria.

El Ejército y las demás iglesias

9. CREEMOS que es voluntad de Dios el establecimiento y desarrollo de relaciones armónicas, por gracia divina, entre todos los cristianos de todas las denominaciones del mundo, incluyendo sus congregaciones locales. Los numerosos contactos que tiene el Ejército con otras comunidades cristianas en todo el mundo contribuyen a su enriquecimiento así como a un mayor conocimiento de la obra del Espíritu Santo. Es por ello que el Ejército acoge este tipo de contactos y aspira cordialmente a su ampliación y profundización.

   NO CREEMOS que la estrechez ni la exclusividad sean consistentes con la voluntad de Dios para con su pueblo, ni que Dios no tenga nada que enseñarnos mediante la relación y cooperación del Ejército con su pueblo de otras denominaciones. A medida que aprendemos con humildad de los demás, venimos también a participar en el banquete ecuménico dispuestos a compartir lo que Dios en su sabiduría y gracia ha encomendado al Ejército.

10. CREEMOS que Dios ha dotado a cada una de las expresiones de la Iglesia universal de sus propias bendiciones y fortalezas. Respetamos y

admiramos esas fortalezas al mismo tiempo que reconocemos que a causa de la fragilidad humana, cada una de esas expresiones, incluyendo el Ejército de Salvación, tiene sus imperfecciones.

NO CREEMOS que nos corresponda expresarnos negativamente ni socavar las tradiciones de las demás denominaciones, y mucho menos en relación con los sacramentos (respecto a los cuales nuestra posición es distinta, aunque no única, y considera que la plenitud de la vida es un sacramento y un llamado de Dios a los salvacionistas a ser testimonios de una vida de santidad sin emplear para ello sacramentos formales). Formular comentarios adversos sobre la vida de cualquier denominación o congregación local va en contra de nuestras prácticas. Tratamos de tener sumo cuidado para no minimizar las doctrinas o prácticas de ningún otro grupo cristiano. El Ejército no enfatiza en su enseñanza los factores externos sino la necesidad que tiene cada creyente de experimentar personalmente una gracia espiritual, al igual presentes en las practicas de otras denominaciones. Afirmamos que ninguna práctica como tal es esencial para la salvación o la recepción de la gracia divina, y que la verdad bíblica es poder conocer a Dios mediante la fe para recibir su gracia en cualquier momento o lugar. Reconocemos que algunas prácticas tales como el bautismo o la eucaristía son empleados por muchas denominaciones para alcanzar la gracia. Creemos que nuestro llamado a la santidad sin la utilización de sacramentos no contradice las prácticas de las demás iglesias, sino que constituye un bello regalo para Cristo lo que ha de entenderse como una paradoja —igual de bellas, pero muy diferentes practicas — de las demás denominaciones. En los designios divinos no hay lugar para las contradicciones inherentes, sino para las paradojas creativas.

11. CREEMOS que el Ejército de Salvación fue levantado por voluntad de Dios, se sostiene por la gracia de Dios y recibe el poder del Espíritu Santo para la obediencia. La esencia de nuestro propósito, concentrada en el nombre que Dios nos ha dado –El Ejército de Salvación– es luchar para guiar a los hombres y mujeres, niños y niñas a una fe salvadora en Jesucristo, obrando sin descanso para Él con el fin de que crezcan en la vida santa, puedan servir mejor a la humanidad sufriente y puedan conservarse limpios de la corrupción del mundo (Santiago 1:26-27).

NO CREEMOS que sólo somos nosotros los llamados a desempeñar estas sagradas y

maravillosas obras, y por eso nos llena de
inmenso regocijo encontrar colaboradores de
Dios en las demás iglesias.

NOTA:

Para detalles acerca de la aceptación
salvacionista de los credos cristianos históricos
(el Credo Apostólico, el Credo Niceno, el
Credo Atanasiano) véase la *Historia de la
Salvación, Manual Salvacionista de Doctrina*
(Ejército de Salvación, Londres, 1998).

Ejército de Salvación
Joven Soldado

Mi Promesa

Habiendo obtenido el perdón de Dios, seré su amante y obediente hijo.

Jesús es mi Salvador personal, confiaré en su poder para guardarme del mal, y tratare de ayudar a otros a seguirle.

Prometo orar, leer mi Biblia y, con su ayuda, vivir una vida limpia en pensamiento, palabra y acción, incluyendo la abstinencia total del uso de tabaco, alcohol y drogas.

PACTO DEL SOLDADO

*Promesas hechas durante el enrolamiento como
soldado del Ejército de Salvación*

Habiendo aceptado a Jesucristo como mi Salvador y
Señor y deseando desempeñar mi calidad de
miembro de Su Iglesia en la tierra como un soldado
del Ejército de Salvación, aquí y ahora, por la gracia
de Dios, contraigo este Pacto sagrado.

Declaro que creo en, y viviré de acuerdo con, las
verdades de la palabra de Dios expresadas en los once
artículos de fe del Ejército de Salvación:
Creemos que las Escrituras del Antiguo y Nuevo
Testamento fueron dadas por inspiración de Dios, y
que sólo ellas constituyen la regla divina de fe y
práctica cristianas

Creemos que hay un solo Dios, quien es
infinitamente perfecto, Creador, Preservador y
Gobernador de todas las cosas y que es a Él sólo a
quien se debe rendir culto religioso.

Creemos que la Deidad se constituye de tres
personas, el Padre, el Hijo y el Espíritu Santo,
indivisas en esencia, e iguales en poder y gloria.

Creemos que en la persona de Jesucristo se unen las naturalezas divina y humana, de tal manera que Él es verdadera y esencialmente Dios y verdadera y esencialmente hombre.

Creemos que nuestros primeros padres fueron creados en estado de inocencia, mas por haber desobedecido perdieron su pureza y felicidad y por efecto de su caída todos los hombres han llegado a ser pecadores, totalmente corrompidos y como tales están con justicia expuestos a la ira de Dios.

Creemos que el Señor Jesucristo, por sus padecimientos y muerte, ha hecho la propiciación por todo el mundo, de manera que todo el que quiera pueda ser salvo.

Creemos que el arrepentimiento para con Dios, la fe en nuestro Señor Jesucristo y la regeneración por el Espíritu Santo, son necesarios para la salvación.

Creemos que somos justificados por gracia mediante la fe en nuestro Señor Jesucristo, y que el que cree tiene el testimonio de ello en sí mismo.

Creemos que el continuar en estado de salvación depende del ejercicio constante de la fe y obediencia a Cristo.

Creemos que es privilegio de todos los creyentes ser santificado "por completo" y que su ser entero, "espíritu, alma y cuerpo", pueden ser guardados "irreprensible para la venida de nuestro Señor Jesucristo". (I Tesalonicenses 5:23).

Creemos en la inmortalidad del alma, en la resurrección del cuerpo, en el juicio general del fin del mundo, en la eterna felicidad de los justos y en el castigo perpetuo de los malos.

Declaración

Declaro que seré sensible a la obra del Espíritu Santo y obediente a Su dirección en mi vida, creciendo en gracia mediante la adoración, la oración, el servicio y la lectura de la Biblia.

Declaro que haré de los valores del Reino de Dios, y no de los valores del mundo, mi norma de vida.

Declaro que mantendré integridad cristiana en cada aspecto de mi vida, rechazando cualquier pensamiento, palabra o acción que pudiera ser impura o indigna, o profana o falsa, deshonesta o inmoral.

Declaro que mantendré ideales cristianos en todas mis relaciones con otros, con mi familia y vecinos, con mis colegas y camaradas salvacionistas, con aquellos ante quienes y por quienes soy responsable, y con la comunidad en general.

Declaro que defenderé la santidad del matrimonio y de la vida familiar.

Declaro que seré fiel administrador de mi tiempo y dones, de mi dinero y posesiones; de mi cuerpo, mi mente y mi espíritu, sabiendo que debo rendir cuenta a Dios.

Declaro que me abstendré del uso de bebidas alcohólicas, del tabaco, de drogas que producen adicción, salvo aquellas prescritas por un médico, de los juegos de azar, la pornografía, las ciencias ocultas, y todo aquello que podría esclavizar mi cuerpo o mi espíritu.

Declaro que seré fiel a los propósitos para los cuales Dios levantó al Ejército de Salvación, compartiendo buenas nuevas de Jesucristo, tratando de ganar a otros para Él y ayudando en Su nombre a los necesitados y a los menos privilegiados.

Declaro que hasta donde me sea posible me comprometeré activamente en la vida y trabajo, culto y testimonio del Cuerpo, contribuyendo con la mayor proporción posible de sus ingresos al sostén de sus ministerios y el trabajo mundial del Ejército de Salvación.

Declaro que seré fiel a los principios y las prácticas del Ejército de Salvación, leal a sus líderes, demostrando un espíritu de salvacionismo tanto en tiempos de popularidad como en tiempos de persecución.

Llamo aquí y ahora a todos los presentes a atestiguar que he contraído este Pacto y firmo estos Artículos de Guerra de mi propia y libre voluntad, convencido que el amor de Cristo, quien murió y ahora vive por salvarme, exige de mi esta devoción de mi vida a su servicio para la salvación del mundo entero y, por lo tanto, declaro aquí mi completa determinación de ser, mediante la ayuda de Dios, un fiel soldado del Ejército de Salvación.

Ejercito de Salvación
Escuela de Entrenamiento
para Oficiales

Mi Pacto

Llamado por Dios a proclamar el Evangelio de nuestro Señor y Salvador Jesucristo, como un oficial del Ejército de Salvación,

Como oficial del Ejército de Salvación me comprometo con Él mediante este solemne pacto:

A servir y amarle por todos mis días, a vivir para ganar almas y hacer de su salvación el propósito supremo de mi vida.

A cuidar de los pobres, alimentar a los hambrientos, vestir al desnudo, amar a los difíciles de amar y ser amigo de los que no tienen amigos.

A mantener las doctrinas y principios de Ejército de Salvación y por gracia de Dios, ser un oficial digno.

Suscrito en la fuerza de mi Señor y Salvador, en presencia del Jefe Territorial, oficiales de la Escuela de Cadetes y mis colegas Cadetes.